I Wonder Why

Kangaroos Have Pouches

and other questions about baby animals

Jenny Wood

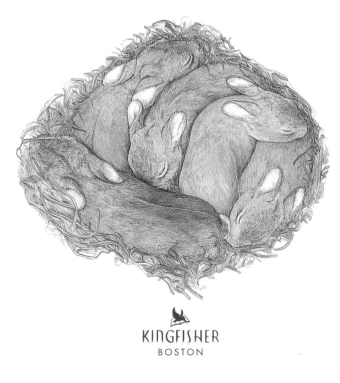

KINGFISHER

BOSTON

KINGFISHER
a Houghton Mifflin Company imprint
222 Berkeley Street
Boston, Massachusetts 02116
www.houghtonmifflinbooks.com

First published in 1996
First published in this format in 2003

10 9 8 7 6 5 4 3 2 1
1TR/0403/SHE/UNV(FR)/126.6MA

LIBRARY OF CONGRESS CATALOGING-IN-PUBLICATION DATA
Wood, Jenny,
I wonder why kangaroos have pouches and other
questions about baby animals / Jenny Wood.
1st ed.
p. cm.—(I wonder why)
Includes index.
Summary: Answers a variety of questions about
baby animals and their parents.
1. Animals—Infancy—Juvenile literature. 2. Parental
behavior in animals—Juvenile literature.
[1. Animals—Infancy. 2. Parental behavior in animals. 3. Questions and answers.]
I. Title. II. Series: I wonder why (New York, N.Y.)
QL763.W66 1996 591.3'9—dc20
96-183 CIP AC

ISBN 0-7534-5661-3

Printed in Taiwan

Editor: Clare Oliver
Series designer: David West Children's Books.
Cover illustration: David Wright (Kathy Jakeman)
Cartoons: Tony Kenyon (B.L. Kearley)
Consultant: Michael Chinery

CONTENTS

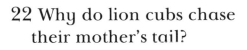

Which baby has the best mother?

A baby gorilla has one of the best moms in the world. A grown-up gorilla may look a bit frightening to us, but she's loving and gentle to her young. As well as grooming the baby, she feeds it for up to three years, and protects and helps it for longer still.

● Gorillas are a type of ape—along with chimpanzees, gibbons, and orangutans. All the apes make very good moms.

Which baby has the worst mother?

The female European cuckoo can't be bothered to take care of her chicks. This lazy mom lays an egg in another bird's nest. When the egg hatches, it's the other bird that does all the hard work, raising the chick.

● The cuckoo manages to trick birds because her egg matches the other ones in the nest.

Which mother has her babies in prison?

When the female hornbill is ready to lay her eggs in a hole in a tree, the male helps block up the door to keep the eggs safe. But he leaves a hole for her beak and feeds her while she's inside!

● Tree shrews are part-time moms. They leave their babies in the nest, only coming by to feed them every other day.

Which father "gives birth" to his young?

The male seahorse has a special pouch on his body where the female lays her eggs. The male then carries them around till they hatch, when hundreds of baby seahorses shoot out into the sea.

Whose feet keep an egg warm?

Every year, in the middle of the winter, a female emperor penguin lays one egg and gives it to her mate to keep warm. He balances the egg between his feet and his feathers, until it hatches in the early spring.

- Male sticklebacks take care of their young. If a baby tries to swim away, the dad grabs it gently in his mouth and spits it back into the nest.

Which father has a chest like a sponge?

Sandgrouse live in the dry desert areas of Africa, Asia, and southern Europe. When water's short, the male flies hundreds of miles to a water hole and soaks up water in his feathers. Then he flies back to his thirsty chicks and lets them suck out the water for a long, refreshing drink.

- Many animal fathers play no part in bringing up their young. Most of them leave before the babies are even born.

Why do kangaroos have pouches?

● Only female kangaroos have pouches. The males don't have babies, so they don't need them!

A pouch is a safe place for a baby to grow. A newborn kangaroo is only the size of a peanut. It struggles through its mom's fur until it reaches her warm pouch. There, it feeds on her milk and goes on growing.

Who hangs on for dear life?

A baby lemur rides on its mom's back for the first seven months of its life. It wraps its legs around her and holds on tightly as she leaps through the trees on a hair-raising ride.

Who's carried by the scruff of the neck?

Like all cat mothers, a leopard lifts her cub by gripping the back of its neck in her teeth. The skin is very loose and baggy here, so the cub isn't hurt. It hangs quite still until she gently puts it down again.

● A female crocodile carries her babies in her mouth, being careful not to bite them with her razor-sharp teeth.

Who likes a ride on the water?

Baby grebes often ride along on their mother's back. They don't have to, though. They're perfectly able to swim on their own!

Which baby has lots of aunts?

As well as having a mother, a baby elephant has lots of aunts. That's because female elephants live in large family groups of up to 50 animals. In fact, a new baby not only has plenty of aunts, it has grandmas, sisters, and cousins too!

Which babies stay in a nursery?

Mara parents leave their babies under ground. To make sure they aren't lonely, lots of families share the same burrow. When a mother drops by to feed her young, she checks up on the other mara babies too.

● When a hippo mother goes off to feed, she leaves her calf with a babysitter!

● Maras live in South America. They're a kind of long-legged guinea pig. Mara parents never join their babies in the burrow. They whistle down the hole and the young come scampering out.

- Bees use nurseries too. The eggs hatch out in a special part of the hive.

Which is the biggest nursery?

- A bat mother has such sharp hearing that she can separate her baby's call from a million others in the cave.

Bracken Cave in Texas is home to over 20 million bats. The mother bats leave their babies in a nursery, huddled together. They are so tightly packed that there may be a thousand in a space the size of a doormat.

What's inside a bird's egg?

There are three things inside a bird's egg—a baby bird, a yellow yolk, and a clear jelly called the white. The yolk is food for the growing bird. The white is food, too, but it also protects the bird if the egg gets a knock.

● Some eggs don't get the chance to hatch. They are eaten by hungry hunters.

● Some eggs hatch quickly, others more slowly. A baby housefly hatches in 24 hours. But a kiwi chick takes three months or more.

● Whale sharks lay the biggest eggs— they're about the size of a baseball.

12

Why do birds turn their eggs?

Birds turn their eggs so that every part of the egg gets its fair share of warmth. The baby birds need warmth to grow—that's why a parent has to sit on the nest.

Is it only birds that lay eggs?

Fish, frogs, snakes, turtles, insects, spiders—all sorts of animals lay eggs. The eggs look and feel quite different. Turtle eggs are soft and leathery, and the size of golf balls. Butterfly eggs are tiny and often sparkle like shiny jewels.

● Caterpillars seem to be born hungry. Many of them gobble up their eggshells as they hatch.

Which baby has the comfiest nest?

Baby rabbits have a nest that is soft and cozy. Their mother builds it inside a burrow, plumping dry grass stalks into a cushion, and then covering it with her own warm fur.

● A baby pack rat isn't as lucky as a rabbit. Its nest is made in a prickly cactus. Ouch!

Which baby is born under the snow?

Polar bear cubs are born in an underground den, which their mother digs deep in the snow. Warm air is trapped inside the den, making it a surprisingly snug place to spend the winter months.

● A hummingbird's nest is about the size of a walnut. It's made from spiders' silk, lichen, flower petals, and plant fluff.

Which nests are 100 years old?

American bald eagles fly back to the same nest year after year. They make a few repairs, then lay their eggs. Some nests are over 100 years old and are bigger and heavier than a car.

● In the United States a pair of woodpeckers made their nest in the space shuttle. They didn't blast off with it though!

Who's at home in a bubble?

Baby froghoppers are often called spittlebugs, because they make a bubbly froth very soon after they're born. They hide in this substance while they feed and grow.

Which is the biggest baby in the world?

The baby blue whale is a real whopper, weighing up to 3 tons—that's as much as 1,000 human babies! As soon as it is born, its mom nudges it to the surface to take a first breath of air.

• A baby blue whale is as long as five scuba divers swimming tip to toe.

• The baby howler monkey is a champion screamer. Its cries can be heard even through thick rain forest.

Which is the tallest baby?

A baby giraffe is about six feet tall—that's taller than most grown-up people. The mother giraffe is taller still and gives birth standing up. Her new baby hits the ground feet first. Ouch!—it's a long way to fall.

● The young dragonfly must be one of the fiercest babies. It lives in rivers and lakes and grabs almost anything that moves with its spiky jaws.

Which is the ugliest baby?

One of the ugliest-looking babies is the vulture chick, with its big hooked beak and bare head and neck. But then, its parents aren't very beautiful either. Maybe it comes from eating all that rotting meat!

Why do pandas have one baby at a time?

A mother giant panda gives her cub so much love and attention that she can only cope with one at a time. By taking care of her cub for a year or more, she is helping to make sure that her baby survives.

● There aren't many pandas in the world. Zookeepers fly their pandas around the world so they can meet other pandas—and hopefully breed.

Which animals lay hundreds of eggs?

Most frogs and toads lay hundreds of eggs in a big frothy mass called spawn. Many of the eggs are eaten, but some of them survive and hatch into tadpoles.

● The giant clam may have the biggest family of all. Every year the female lays a great cloud of eggs—a billion or more!

Which family is always identical?

Each time a nine-banded armadillo gives birth, she has four identical babies. They are either all female or all male. This is because a single egg inside the mother splits into four, and all four parts begin to grow—into identical quadruplets!

● Albatross moms lay just one egg every two years. Both parents take care of the chick for about ten months until it's big enough to fly.

Which baby drinks the creamiest milk?

A mother harp seal's milk is so thick and rich that it looks more like mayonnaise than milk. It's about 12 times creamier than cow's milk and is such good food that you can almost see the harp seal pup growing fatter as it feeds!

• A seal pup has to grow quickly so that its mother can go off and catch fish. She spends three weeks just feeding her pup—after that she's starving!

• Many seal pups are born in the coldest parts of the world. But they don't freeze to death because they have a thick layer of fat covered with a furry coat to keep them nice and warm.

Which parent serves meals in a bag?

● A baby salmon hatches with its own lunchbox! The tiny fish has a pouch of food, a bit like an egg yolk, that keeps it going for several weeks.

The pelican has a baggy pouch of skin under its beak, which it uses to scoop up fish. Then it drains off the water and swallows them all. When a chick needs feeding, the parent brings up a mouthful of fish and lets the baby feed from the pouch. Yummy!

● The polyphemus moth caterpillar must be one of the hungriest babies. In the first 56 days of its life, it munches 86,000 times its own birthweight in leaves. That's like a human baby eating six large truckloads of food!

● The insides of many baby birds' mouths are brightly colored. People think that this encourages the parents to feed the hungry chicks.

Why do lion cubs chase their mother's tail?

Lion cubs are very playful, and pounce on anything that moves—especially the tassel on the end of their mom's tail. Games like this teach the cubs how to chase and pounce—skills they'll need when they have to hunt for themselves.

● Sea otters know how to have fun. The mother tosses her baby into the air and then catches it again. Wheeee!

● Play is how baby animals learn all sorts of important skills for grown-up life.

Why do ducklings play follow-the-leader?

When ducklings hatch, they follow the first moving thing they see, which is usually their mother. By following her everywhere, they learn how to swim and feed. And if they wander off, she only has to call and they fall in line!

● Some parents teach their young how to use tools. Baby chimps soon learn how to dig for termites with a stick.

● Bear cubs learn from their mother how to catch fish. They scoop them out of the river with their paws.

When does a puppy grow into a dog?

Every puppy is blind and helpless when it's born, but by the time it's two years old it will be fully grown. All pups are roughly the same size when they're born, whatever the type of dog. No wonder it takes smaller types of dogs less time to finish growing up!

2 By six weeks, the puppy is starting to explore. It plays with its brothers and sisters and enjoys a tumble!

1 At about two weeks, the puppy's eyes and ears open. It will begin walking soon.

● A baby wildebeest runs before it can walk! The youngster trots along beside its mother just five minutes after it's born.

When does a tiger cub leave home?

A mother tiger takes care of her cubs until they're about two years old. But then she has another litter and ignores the older cubs. It's not really cruel— the two-year-olds are grown now, and it's about time they took care of themselves.

3 By the time it is full grown, the dog is strong and active. Good food and exercise will help it to stay fit.

● Most insects change shape as they grow. A beetle starts life as a wriggly larva. Then it turns into a pupa. It may not look like it's doing much, but inside the hard skin the insect is changing fast. When it crawls out, it's a full-grown beetle.

Larva　　**Pupa**　　**Beetle**

Which baby hides in the forest?

A young deer, called a fawn, is very wobbly on its legs. It cannot outrun a hungry cougar or wolf! So when it senses danger the young animal freezes and stays completely still until the danger has passed. The fawn's speckled coat helps it seem almost invisible in the soft, forest's dappled light.

Which babies hide in a circle of horns?

Adult musk oxen make a circle around their calves when danger threatens. They stand close together with their heads lowered, facing the enemy like a row of shields. It takes a very brave wolf to attack the wall of long, curved horns!

- Lots of animals make noises to scare away enemies. Young burrowing owls, which live in holes in the ground, can make a noise like a rattlesnake when they are threatened.

Which mother pretends she's sick?

If a hungry hunter threatens a plover's nest, the mother plover pretends to be wounded. She flaps a wing as if it were broken and flutters weakly along the ground—away from the nest. She wants the enemy to think that because she is injured she can be easily captured. That way, the predator will go after her, not her babies.

- A mother scorpion protects her young for the first few days of their lives by carrying them on her back. If an enemy approaches, she arches her poison-tipped tail high above her back. That'll usually stop the enemy from coming any closer!

Which baby is always being washed?

A mother cat licks her kittens from the moment they're born. Licking roughly around the newborn kitten's mouth makes it gasp and start breathing. The mother's tongue dries the kitten's fur too, to keep the kitten warm.

● Flamingos preen their chick's feathers as well as their own. They pick out dirt and insects, and spread oil over the feathers. This oil is produced by the bird's own glands, and makes the feathers waterproof.

● Mud might not seem like a good thing to clean yourself with, but there is nothing a baby hippo likes more than a wallow in a mud bath! And, believe it or not, the mud protects the hippo's skin from the sun and keeps it soft.

Who enjoys a grooming?

A baboon makes sure her babies are well groomed. Working slowly, section by section, she parts the baby's fur and picks carefully with her fingers. She will remove pieces of dead skin, insects, and dirt—and most of what she finds, she eats!

● Sometimes a foal snaps at its mother, but it's only being friendly! The "biting" action is the foal's way of asking its mother to nuzzle it and groom its coat.

Which baby lives in the cleanest nest?

Lots of animals keep their babies' nests clean, but the badger would probably win first prize! Adult badgers regularly line their burrows with fresh dried grass and leaves. They even dig special holes well away from the burrow, which the whole family uses as toilets.

OCCUPIED

How does a lamb find its mother?

CLICK CLICK

Mother sheep and their lambs sometimes get separated in a crowded field. Most lambs look the same but each one has its own distinctive call. Every mother sheep knows her own baby's cry and can easily find it in the crowd.

• Most whales and dolphins talk to their young and to each other using clicks, grunts, and other sounds. A baby humpback can hear its mother up to 100 miles away, so it can never get lost!

• A mother moose nudges her baby from behind. This tells the young moose that it has to keep moving on, even if it is feeling tired.

Which baby gets smacked when it's naughty?

When a baby elephant is naughty, its mother punishes her calf by whacking it with her trunk. The baby learns quickly what it should and should not do! But a mother elephant will also use her trunk to stroke her baby and other young elephants in the herd. This is a sign of affection.

● Wolf cubs learn to howl by copying the sounds their parents make.

● The manatee nuzzles her young and cradles it in her flippers to prevent it from floating away in the current.

Index